THE HUMAN MALE

A MEN'S LIBERATION DRAFT POLICY

BY HARVEY JACKINS AND OTHERS

A few years ago, some of the leaders in the Re-evaluation Counseling (RC) movement realized that not only are men mistreated (as all people in current societies are), but that men are also specifically *oppressed as men*.

A considerable amount of thought and discussion has since taken place within RC about the nature of men's oppression and actions to be taken about it.[1] Until now, however, there has been no comprehensive program for the *liberation of men*.[2] This document is intended to serve as a basis for a discussion of the world-wide situation for men, an introduction to the processes of discharge and re-evaluation for those men who are not already acquainted with them, and a framework for a men's liberation movement.[3]

SOCIETAL AND INSTITUTIONALIZED OPPRESSIONS

The one surviving species of human beings seems superficially to have solved its problems of survival in that

---

[1] Oppression is the systematic mistreatment of a group of people by the society and/or by another group of people who serve as agents of the society, with the mistreatment encouraged or enforced by the society and its culture.

[2] "Liberation" refers to the program and process of freeing one's self and one's group from oppression.

[3] "Discharge" is a term used to collectively describe the various complex physical processes which accompany the release of tension from distress recordings of hurtful experiences, including physical pain, discomfort, or emotional distress. These releasing processes are dependably indicated by the physical manifestations of yawning, stretching, or scratching; sobbing, crying, shedding tears; shaking, trembling, perspiration from a cold skin; perspiration from a warm skin; laughter; shouting; violent physical activity (stamping, pounding); interested talking; relaxed talking; reluctant, bored talking (particularly when accompanied by yawns); and "eager," excited recounting of experiences.

"Re-evaluation" refers to the process, which occurs spontaneously after discharge, through which distress recordings are understood and turned into usable information.

the planet is currently supporting a very large number of its members (six billion and growing). A closer look, however, makes it plain that the very "success" of our massive reproduction rate is threatening disaster for ourselves and the rest of the marvelous planet on which we have arisen.

The size of the human population in itself is not the source of the problem, however. The basic problem is that our species has not been able to deal with the fact that we function in two completely different modes: In the first mode, we rely on the use of our flexible, creative intelligence. In the second mode, we behave unintelligently, because our intelligence has been interfered with by an accumulation of rigid distress patterns which have been left upon us from individual experiences of being hurt.[4] This non-intelligent mode has led to the development of class societies[5] and other oppressive structures, which are dominated by and promote patterns of selfish, greedy exploitation. The oppressive societies, in their turn, install, maintain, and enforce unintelligent rigid behaviors on each new generation of humans.

It is crucial that as many of us as possible make the move to functioning on the basis of our intelligence rather than on the basis of distress recordings.[6] We need

---

[4] "Intelligence" as used here refers to the ability to create a new, successful, creative response to fit each new, present situation. "Distress pattern" refers to a rigid set of "thoughts," behaviors, and feelings that is left by an undischarged experience (or experiences) of distress.

[5] "Class societies" refer to the structuring of society where one group of people oppresses (exploits) another and has greater access to the resources of that society with the rationalized argument of better organization for production. There are three kinds of class societies: slave societies, feudal societies, and capitalist societies.

[6] "Distress recording" refers to all the information (sights, smells, voice-tones, gestures, postures, feelings, etc.) that gets bound together in an unusable glob during a distress experience and then is played over and over (like a record) in an inappropriate response to a similar-enough new situation.

to begin to think about our total environment with as much care and devotion and effort as we have ever in the past turned on any beloved individual. Defense of our environment is crucial for the very survival and existence of life in general.

One of the basic discoveries of Re-evaluation Counseling (RC) is that the rigid, unintelligent patterns with which we have become infested can be eliminated. The key element in the recovery process is the discharge of physical and emotional distresses and subsequent re-evaluation, leading to recovery of intelligent, flexible functioning. This discovery is of crucial importance to the project of ensuring that intelligence determines the future of our species and our planet.

All groups of humans in our present societies tend to be conditioned against the discharge and re-evaluation process, but this conditioning[7] falls with special intensity upon males, with the result that men are particularly set up to be agents for the continuation of class societies and all other oppressions.

Some of the verbal conditionings which have been put upon men, such as "big boys don't cry," "don't be a scaredy cat," "be a man," "it's a man's job to die for his country," begin in the very first moments of men's lives. These patterns not only begin to ruin the lives of males immediately, but also set them up to unintelligently accept and perpetrate the oppressions of all people. In most societies, the process of growing from boyhood to manhood is beset by a deliberate discouragement and suppression of men's abilities to feel their own emotions and to discharge the distressed ones. Fear, grief, loneliness, and uncertainty are often covered over with a

---

[7] "Conditioning" is the psychological term for interrupting the free thinking of an individual by imposing a pattern which leaves the individual inhibited from acting on his or her own thinking and under pressure to succumb to the demands of other individuals.

pretense of "confidence." For many men, the isolation that results from early violence, threats of violence, and harsh expectations of "what it is to be a man" leaves them literally unable to recognize, admit, and feel their feelings. This conditioning is one of the elements that forces men to play the often inhuman roles they are expected to play in our oppressive societies, be it in relation to women, to themselves, to children, or to society as a whole. (This is because undischarged distress creates a compulsion to replay the original hurt, sometimes in the victim role—as in the original incident—but often in the perpetrator role.) For all men to recover the ability and freedom to "feel their feelings" and not only "feel" but *discharge* their *distressed* feelings, and so recover their intelligence, is a key survival process that needs support from all men, and from all humans.

All humans claiming intelligence and goodwill need to make a frontal attack on the intensively organized suppression of little boys' natural ability to discharge. We need to say clearly and dramatically to parents and teachers that any small child (female as well as male) can, with persistent, informed support, be protected to emerge as an outstanding individual, universally celebrated for his or her brilliant qualities. We need to call for and launch organizational efforts to see to it that parents, schools, and religious institutions are informed and organized to stop the damage to males at the little-boy stage and to continue to protect them as they grow older so that they can be boldly and powerfully intelligent, kind, and effective.

Men, like all human beings, are inherently good, caring, gentle, and warm. Their excellent real nature is obscured and apparently distorted by the heavy conditioning society puts upon them, but it remains undestroyed and recoverable. Men's *inherent* attitude, as men, is to oppose and prevent any enforced inequalities with regard to life, liberty, and the pursuit of happiness, and to support all efforts toward liberation from oppression. As human males, they inherently strive to achieve and provide universal access to information and to the basic resources needed by all living things. It is an honor to be a man and, as such, to be able to lend resource, leadership, strength, information, and nurture to *every* person's struggle against enforced inequality, regardless of age, gender, background, or previous experience. The abundant examples of men acting in these ways in all eras and places are not exceptions, but show men's true inherent nature.

Though males, like all humans, are by nature cooperative and caring, there is a widespread belief in most human cultures at present that boys and men are by nature violent or aggressive. This belief leaves boys alone with many struggles and paves the road for later, increased violence and aggression. When boys act violently, it must never be assumed that "all is normal." *Boys are never violent or aggressive except as a result of having been brutalized.*

Some other mistaken notions widespread in present cultures are that boys "don't need" to be held and nurtured in the same way that girls do, or that there's a goodness and innocence present in women that is absent in men, or that it's good for boys to hurt and suffer the hurts alone in order to "harden" them in preparation for manhood. Some other widely believed nonsense is that men don't feel pain as much as women do, or that men are inherently compulsive sexually. None of these are true, and all of these need to be exposed and eliminated.

Until recently, most discussion in our societies about men's difficulties has been focused on concern about men's tendency toward "criminal or anti-social behavior." In recent years, some attention has been given to issues relating to men and health. As we reach for greater awareness in this area, we are forced to realize that men have fared and fare very badly. Men die younger than women. Men commit suicide more often than women almost everywhere in the world, up to nine times as often in some countries (and these numbers are increasing).[8] Men still make comparatively little use of medical services (and very little of the health information made public is aimed at men). Men have the highest rates of alcohol and other drug addictions, and of sexually-transmitted diseases.

With any other group, such figures would be taken as reliable indications that the group in question is oppressed.

Still, our society acts reluctant to recognize men as an oppressed group. The emphasis in the society is on men as agents of all oppressions. Yet thoughtful examination of the situation has led us in RC to conclude that men are indeed *oppressed*.

There is no designated group of people assigned by the oppressive society to carry out the oppression of males. (This is different from the situation with some other oppressions, in which a particular group is "trained and assigned" to be in the oppressive role relative to another group. For example, whites are "trained and assigned" to install and perpetuate racism—the oppression of people of color. Men are "trained and assigned" to install and perpetuate sexism—the oppression of females.)

In carrying out the oppression of men, the society as a whole plays the role of the oppressor. Nearly everyone in our societies plays some role in men's oppression, and nearly everyone has rigid attitudes and "beliefs" that are oppressive to men. It will be essential in ending men's oppression to change these widely held attitudes and be-

---

[8] World Health Organization statistics

liefs. It helps in the task of clarifying the situation, and organizing to change it, if we identify particular institutions as the agents of men's oppression.

THE *INSTITUTIONS* OF MEN'S OPPRESSION

There are several well-organized institutions that operate to install and perpetuate the oppression of men. These institutions' functions are usually characterized as "social," and some of them do indeed perform social functions in other ways, but even casual observation of their operation makes it plain that each of them plays a major role in constructing dehumanized versions of what a man is, and in disempowering and exploiting men.

Some of them are organized primarily to target males. This institutionalized concentration on oppressing men was often much plainer in past generations. In the name of "women's liberation," there has been some blurring of appearances in recent years, as the oppressing institutions have reached out to extend their contamination to females (often in the name of "fairness"). However, in this document we will focus on the impact of each of these institutions on males, and will propose actions to be taken to remedy these effects.

Before discussing in detail the institutions that oppress men, we need to look at the way the oppression of males is "internalized."

INTERNALIZED OPPRESSION

One of the results of the external, institutional oppression is the creation of distress recordings. This means that the person who has been oppressed carries around recordings of *feeling oppressed* which, when restimulated,[9] act upon him or her to produce feelings as if fresh oppression was coming from outside, even if no new

---

[9] "Restimulation" refers to the "replaying" of a recording of a hurtful experience, which is brought on by a perceived similarity (sometimes insignificant or remote) in the current situation to the past hurtful situation.

oppression is taking place. This is "internalized oppression," and it operates so as to have the man believe the negative stereotypes of men. Past invalidations have the effect on the man as if they were still being received and currently invalidating him.

Internalized oppression is the most insidious difficulty facing any oppressed group, and men are no different in this regard. Most of the difficulties endured by men are caused by male internalized oppression. These recordings, when restimulated, leave the man on whom the recordings have been made feeling discouraged, isolated, guilty, depressed, angry, and vulnerable to interacting with other men's negative recordings in mutual hostility, disappointment, etc.

The most effective means for contradicting men's internalized oppression is to find ways for men to become intelligent parts of each other's lives—to show their flexible, warm, mutually-appreciative selves to each other.[10]

To achieve this goes to the root of the isolation internalized by individual men, makes it impossible for internalized oppression to drive men to hurt each other, and rocks the foundations of institutionalized men's oppression. For men to make close friends with other men is to enable them to become aware of the conditioning that has been put upon them and to want liberation from it. As men reach for friendship with men from different class backgrounds, different cultures, and so on, they will inevitably deepen and enrich their awareness of, and their intense desire for, liberation.

It may sometimes appear difficult to directly raise the issue of men's oppression. The main reason for this apparent difficulty is that men's stories *have not been*

---

[10] "Contradict" usually refers to "contradicting distress," meaning helping the client to see that the distress recording is not present-time reality.

told—the "real" stories, that is, not just the "public" versions permitted by the oppression. When the real stories are told, then the real issues become clearer. Organizing men's groups in which men "take turns listening" to each other is a basic necessity for men's liberation.

Men need to reclaim an unshakable understanding of their own inherent goodness. At present most men struggle to even *notice* that they don't know they are *completely* good. This is a major obstacle to their quest to find ways to discharge the internalized oppression.

Being seen as the "bad ones" in society leaves men little room for recovery from their hurts. We have learned that, in many ways, the young person whose distress leads him (or her) to harm another young person can suffer more from the act than the recipient of that act. The one who has been hit on the head with the toy truck can be crying and receiving attention, while the one who did the deed can be abandoned in feeling bad and guilty. The other people around are most often (even when they know and understand RC theory) confused about the goodness of the one who did the hitting. Under these conditions, it is very hard for someone who acts out a distress to discharge on it. When a boy shows by an "unacceptable" act how he has been hurt, and receives disapproval, punishment, violence, and the reproaches of others, he has been pounded into a tight corner—even more so if the disapproval is expressed as blame for "being a boy." This is the situation for many men.

The liberation of women and of men go hand in hand. Because men have been used as the oppressor group toward women (through the systematic installation of *sexist* patterns, beginning very early in boys' lives), they need to deal specifically with the damage done to women by sexism. While it is not men's fault that they have been set up to be the oppressor group over women, men cannot afford any tolerance toward continuing to play that role.

The slightest oppressive act is completely unworthy of men's inherent excellence. Explicit renunciation of that role and the correction of it by eliminating any sexism anywhere in society falls logically to men. Not only can men throw off the oppressor role, they can also work to eliminate sexism from society and assist women to eliminate the women's internalized sexism.[11]

In the present human population of approximately six billion people and in the probably huge emerging population of the next decades, support of the female gender as a whole is tremendously important to all humans. Large numbers of women world-wide still die in childbirth, lack adequate medical care and food during pregnancy, give birth to children who quickly become malnourished and ill, and receive little support from the men around them. This will change as present oppressions are ended, as modern science increases the possible choices before women, and as reproduction of the species becomes a question of free choice by individuals. But in all existing levels of society, a vital responsibility is still enforced upon women by their unavoidable role in the reproduction of the species. Currently, for simple survival of the species, ending the oppression of sexism is necessary. Assuming extra care and responsibility for support of women during reproduction and child rearing becomes a basic responsibility of men and, of course, of all humans.

---

[11] "Oppressor role" refers to the role of agreeing to carry out oppression. The person in the oppressor role has always been oppressed first. No one is able to assume the oppressor role without having been extremely mistreated themselves as preparation.

TOWARDS A GENERAL PROGRAM
OF ENDING MEN'S OPPRESSION

Long-term Goal

Our long-term goal is to completely end the oppression of men. This will require eliminating or transforming the institutions that carry out men's oppression, and replacing them with rational human organizations. A central part of this will be to assist all men to reclaim the discharge process. Supportive of this, it will be necessary to assist all people to arrive at an accurate view of the nature of men and to distinguish men's distress patterns from men's inherent goodness. On the way to this goal it will be necessary to engage men in eliminating sexism and all other oppressions of any humans. On a broad front, we will need to replace any part of human society that can be shown to be oppressive.

Strategies

a) Encourage and organize wide discussion of the nature of men's oppression and its existence as an *oppression*. Show how the present class system operates to harm all humans and serves as the basis for all oppressions, including men's oppression. Learn how to oppose and eliminate the oppression of men in every form that it exists. This will require organized activity. *Organize* to end men's oppression.

b) Encourage men to speak out about what life has really been like for them. Publish stories, articles, and interviews with men about their lives, including the experiences of every variety of men in these publications. Organize thousands of men's support groups on an RC basis, with the intent of introducing men to the existence of internalized oppression and the tools and processes available to discharge it.[12]

c) Promote widespread understanding that what the general population has come to think of as the "negative qualities of men" are actually distress recordings that result from men's oppression. Reject the widespread belief in society that boys and men are by nature violent or aggressive, and instead promote the understanding that males are inherently cooperative and caring. Ensure that boys are never raised in violent environments and never required to choose between hurting someone else or being hurt themselves. Train parents and caretakers of boys in helping boys to discharge any feelings of aggression. Train them to know the difference between patterns of violence or aggression and a male's inherent, energetic humanness, and to see any aggressive patterns as a boy's attempt to get help with his distresses.

d) Organize in every way to restore men's sense of their own goodness and worth. Work to eliminate all societal stereotypes that deny this truth and to eradicate or transform all institutions that oppress men and thereby

---

[12] "Support group" refers to an organizational form which first evolved in Re-evaluation Counseling but which now has spread widely in the world. It consists of a group of people of indeterminate size (could be three to fifty) but probably optimally of around eight people, which meets together on the basis of some commonality between members. People take turns being listened to with a rough agreement having been reached of there being approximately the same amount of time for each person's turn. A stringently organized support group will allow each person to use the turn the way that person wishes and will require him or her to end the turn when the agreed-upon time is up. A common form of the support group is one in which a designated person serves as a counselor to each person having a turn. The designated person may be the person agreed-upon to be the leader of the group. Alternatively, each person may choose a different counselor for his or her turn, or agree ahead of time on the order in which other members of the group will serve as counselors. A useful feature of the support group is that at the end of the meeting, and after the time and place of the next meeting are set, each person says what he or she liked best about the meeting as a whole.

leave recordings that men are dispensable, irrelevant, unfeeling, etc. Validate every boy's and man's inherent nature as good in every way.

e) Adapt social environments to accommodate the reality that men are human beings *who have feelings*. Schools, homes, playgrounds, workplaces—all need to be set up so that males are allowed to relax and openly show their feelings and share their thoughts without threats of isolation, intimidation, loss of closeness, or loss of self-esteem. No institution should be permitted to require that men suppress feelings or suppress discharge in order to function.

f) Organize all men to assume primary responsibility for eliminating sexist oppression from the world. Begin by rejecting the notion that there is any difference in the human qualities held by men and women. Insist that each gender is courageous, tender, bold, nurturing, etc. Expose sexism as a hurtful, limiting factor in both men's and women's lives by giving men the chance to discharge on their own hurts and to listen to women's personal experiences of being oppressed by sexism. Include the elimination of sexism as a part of every program for men's liberation.

g) Inside RC, organize large numbers of men's support groups. Multiply the number of men's leaders' groups, hold more men's workshops, and work toward the goal of having fifty percent men in every RC Community. Recruit women to support this process. Men's support groups should become "men's *liberation* groups." Our aggressively-pursued aim should be to change men's lives, not just to comfort one another in discussion groups.

h) Assist all men to discharge, act outside of, and eliminate every form of oppression that tries to divide them from other men. Form deep friendships with men of every class, nationality, age, race, and culture.

13

i) Introduce RC widely, making sure the tools of RC are available to men of all ages, all nationalities, all walks of life. In teaching RC, specifically address the suppression of the discharge process in men and boys in particular, and the connection of the suppression of discharge to men's oppression. Encourage the formation of support groups, for both men and women, which are working to end men's oppression and working to assist men to reclaim the discharge process.

THE PRINCIPAL INSTITUTIONS WHICH CARRY ON THE OPPRESSION OF MEN

The principal institutions which carry on the oppression of males are:

- the armed services
- the criminal courts, police, and prisons
- the workplace exploitation of men as workers
- the "sex industries"
- the alcohol, tobacco, pharmaceutical, and illegal drug industries
- the "sports industries"
- schools
- religions
- the family

There is a relationship among these institutions. All of these institutions in some way serve the functioning of the economic system by which wealth is transferred from the working majority of the population to the owning-class minority of the population. This transfer is accomplished through the use of some legal structures or custom or through long-established, undisguised greed.

The owning classes of different nations compete for the "right" to exploit natural resources and markets. They often resort to military action and war to protect their "national interests." The workplace is the vehicle for creating and accumulating wealth, as the value produced by working people is largely placed in the hands of the owning-class institutions. The working-class majority of people would not agree to be exploited if not for the threats hanging over them from the criminal "justice" system. The addictive "power" of the sports, drug, and sex industries acts to keep the individual workers addicted. Schools, religions, and families are the channels and the places where the message about "what it is to be a man" is formulated and taught, and where people are trained and re-trained for participation in the system and for submission to it.

A. The Armed Services

The most destructive of these institutions is the armed services. Men's oppression makes possible a military establishment, and a military establishment makes possible massive oppression of large numbers of people by small numbers of people through war and the threat of war. While talking about the armed services as a key institution in the oppression of men, we have first to discuss, and deal with, war, the mass destruction of human lives by war, and the enormous environmental damage war involves.

The owning classes of oppressive societies have inevitably, up until now, gone to war as the result of the operation of their economic competition: war has been a process of imperial plundering. There has never been a real necessity for war. Armed human struggle has *no* pro-human role. It is completely *wrong*. Armed struggle is *the* most destructive phenomenon threatening intelligence, humanity, and the future of the world. *There is no **good** war.* If even one war or one armed service is tolerated, it is possible to misuse that tolerance to "justify" others, but this is a false "justification." There have been periods in human history without any wars. Wars are not a natural or necessary part of human existence.

War is *the* great evil, *the* great unintelligent activity. If we are intelligent, we have to be against war, against anything that leads to war, against anything that supports war. Even in times of peace, the traumatizing effects of past wars are still experienced. The maintenance of armed services has destructive effects that ripple throughout societies, including the diversion of labor and resource from real human needs. Total elimination of all militarism is the essence of intelligence.

War and armed struggle impinge on men as *the armed services*. In the armed services themselves, men overwhelmingly are required to kill or be killed in the name of "patriotism," "honor," and "bravery," but the effects extend to all males. The expectation that to be a man is to kill or be killed is almost universal. The standard practice of raising boys to be soldiers is completely dehumanizing. Military training of men strips men of personal identity.

There is nothing noble or heroic about war, yet films and stories (with a few notable exceptions) glamorize it. The toy industries make profits out of selling replicas of weapons to boys who, when they start school, are coerced into competitive sports in preparation for the ultimate competition—war. The armed services use these lies to seduce "impressionable" young men into enlisting, in their hopes that they will thereby accomplish something meaningful or escape from poverty. After wars there is a lot of glamorizing hype about the young men who "went with songs into battle," died "with their faces to the foe," "gave their lives for their country," and so on, whereas the reality was that these men were robbed of their lives and often died in the most horrible and agonizing circumstances.

The defensive role of the military (sometimes called the "defensible part") can be handled more safely and more democratically using non-violent civilian-based actions.[13] A successful example of civilian-based defense is the occasion when France invaded the Ruhr after World War I. The German government told the citizens to not cooperate in any way with the invaders. The French pulled out after several months, humiliated that a military occupation was not sufficient to operate the regional infrastructure.

The military is a flagrant example of class oppression in action: officers act as the upper class; non-commissioned officers act as a middle class; other ranks are treated as the working class or the raised-poor (chronically on welfare) class. Non-commissioned officers do the dirty work of officers (bullying and verbally abusing the men) in return for small privileges, such as higher pay and separate messes. The men are told that thinking, and using their own initiative, are forbidden and that their role is just to "obey orders." There is blatant exploitation of fear in the training so that when ordered to attack, the men fear the military police behind them as much as they do the "enemy" in front.

Most societies refuse to recognize the disastrous effects that going to war has on men and their families. The psychological effect of preparing for war, killing other human beings, being wounded, having close friends die, and many other hurts, must not be underestimated. A survivor's guilt, rage, self-loathing, and destructiveness tend to be acted out on himself, on his spouse, on children, and in other relationships. Many societies, unable to deal with the horrors carried by veterans returning from their war experiences (be they "victorious" or not), choose instead to glorify the heroics of soldiers and to

---

[13] See Gene Sharp's book, *Making Europe Unconquerable.*

minimize their difficulties. Such distortions, if not addressed, have a tremendous social cost, including suicide, addictions, loss of relationships, violence, and lack of productivity. Furthermore, by not addressing the problems of returning veterans, societies hide the horrors of wars, thus making it easier to attempt to "justify" future wars and war preparations.

It is important that the dedicated, caring, and completely good men and women of the armed services not be confused with "the military" as an oppressive institution. Without violence or the threat of violence, soldiers would not be necessary—or possible. Clearly, it is the institution and the distress that it engenders that leads to the destructive hostilities, not the human being in uniform.

Wars for liberation may appear to be an exception. They may be called "justifiable conflicts" since liberation movements often have to begin with violent resistance to already existing armies of repression. The existing armies are committed by their reactionary programs to keep the population repressed by violence and the use of arms, behind the facade of nationalism, patriotism, "anti-communism," and the other well-propagandized, long-established, and glamorized slogans. But even in "wars of liberation," the real long-term gain comes not through the armed conflict (whether "successful" or not), but through patient explanation of where the real interests of the population lie and effective organizing around these interests (winning the "hearts and minds" of people).

GOALS

End war and the armed services, world-wide, for all time. Create all necessary changes in society to ensure that war and military service are ended.

STRATEGIES

a) Launch a world-wide program for the *complete* abolition of war and the complete abolition of armed combat.

18

Don't wait for someone else to start it. "First person singular" not only must start it, but can.

b) Expose and organize against the institutions that support the armed services and war. Expose greed as the (barely) hidden motive behind all military activity. Expose the profiteering of the arms industry. Eliminate the arms industry. End the glamorization and valorization of war.

c) Provide real solutions for the difficulties that people put forth as the justification for armed conflict; let no rationalized justification of armed service as an institution remain unchallenged. Implement rational solutions to human conflicts. These must take into account oppression, the real nature of human beings, and the understanding that there is no inherent conflict between any two humans or any two groups of humans. Explore and publicize alternative ways of filling the defensive and civil roles up to now claimed to have been filled by the military.

d) Expose the real toll that war and military service takes on men (and women). Make public the real stories of members of the armed forces, the true experts on war, and do it most immediately to very young men. Develop comprehensive programs for all veterans of wars. Every man who has been exposed to the war system in any way needs the best help that society can offer him to recover from the atrocities he has witnessed, participated in, and endured. Encourage men (and women) into considering complete non-cooperation with armed service, and speaking out about their choice.

B. The Criminal Courts, Police, and Prisons

Next to the viciousness of the military in the oppression of men, stand the criminal courts, the police, and the prisons.

It is important to recognize that the pretext or excuse used to try to justify these institutions is the one of protecting society from people who have acquired distress patterns, the acting out of which sometimes poses a danger to other people or to society. There are large numbers of committed people who have devoted their lives to trying to make the criminal "justice" system rational-appearing and more workable. Their goal has often been to help the people caught up within the system, who are predominantly men, resist the playing out of these dangerous compulsive patterns and thereby stop them from harming others through their compulsions, and eventually free these people from these patterns.

However, these rational intentions have been overwhelmed and largely negated by the oppressive functioning of the system itself. The actual legal structure of the present oppressive societies primarily preys upon men, threatens men, and exploits them. It does this by presenting a vast collection of fictions about men to try to secure their submission to the oppressive structure of the society itself and to enforce the class position in which the society has placed them. Overwhelmingly this is done to working-class men, but middle-class and owning-class men also find that legal structures have been devised to force them "back into line" if their human intelligence tempts them to resist the oppressive positions assigned to them.

Within prisons, all other oppressions, particularly racism and classism, are relatively undisguised and particularly harsh.[14] The criminal "justice" system is par-

---

[14] "Classism" refers to the economic exploitation of one group of people by another. One group of people who produce value by their work have that value taken away from them by another group of people, with the robbery organized and supported by the society. This economic exploitation, this taking of the wealth produced by some people away from them by others, is the whole motivation of class societies. It is therefore the fundamental oppression.

ticularly vicious in its effects on men from groups targeted by white racism, such as African-American men or Aboriginal men (in Australia, where the number of Aboriginal deaths in custody is a glaring indictment of the murderous system). For many communities of color, incarceration has been so much a part of men's lives that it has come to be seen by many young men as a "rite of passage" into "manhood."

Many people are under the impression that prisons hold a large number of men with violent patterns, who are "dangerous." Creating such an impression seems to have been a deliberate attempt to use fear to justify cooperation with oppressive measures. The actual situation is quite manageable if it were faced with a rational program. In United States federal prisons, only eleven percent of inmates are there for violent crime (homicide, rape, manslaughter, robbery, aggravated assault, and simple assault). Only six percent of those imprisoned in a recent year were imprisoned for violent offenses.[15]

The prison system, far from working to assist men, instead brutalizes them and pushes them into becoming "more efficient" criminals. No man should ever be isolated, blamed, punished, or executed for his difficulties. Regardless of a man's behavior, a man must never be scapegoated for the difficulties of society as a whole.

"Punishment" is held out by the oppressive society as a remedy and correction for misbehavior or misfunctioning. Actually, the misfunctioning was caused in the first place by distress that interfered with the person's thinking clearly, and the punishment increases the distress and increases the likelihood of more misfunctioning. It may lead the "offender" to deny any responsibility or conceal his misfunction, or resort to

---

[15] The United States is the most incarceration-prone Western "democracy." Good information about the prison and criminal justice system can be found in *The Real War on Crime* (1996) Donziger.

violence to try to escape society's further "punishment" of him, but the more distress that is added to the "offender" by punishment, the more likely the person is to misfunction out of confusion, and as the amount of tension increases, by compulsion. If the person can be treated with friendliness and kindness and listened to, it tends to make it possible for the person to think through the distress (which he is really anxious to be freed from) and be able to correct his behavior as a result of discharge. Any punishment makes this harder to do and tends to guarantee persistence in "crime."

The idea that a person should ever be subject to the death penalty or execution is **wrong!** The understanding we now have, that punishment exacerbates misbehavior and that a person can be completely freed from distress recordings, completely negates any previous "justifications" for the death penalty. The value to society of any intelligent human is certainly up in the billions of dollars (if you count the cost of creating a complex organism that can actually think intelligently). That our society accepts the destruction of such an elegant organism is dangerous to its own survival.

In many parts of the world, prisons are warehouses for men whose violent or lonely lives have driven them to the fringes of society. Prisons are also used to scapegoat men for society's failures, particularly poverty, class inequality, and racism. Many men are imprisoned for the "crimes" they commit while hungry, scared, lonely, sick, or standing up against injustice. Being unemployed and living on the streets (being a "vagabond," being a "vagrant") is a crime in most modern societies.

The current criminal-law systems of many societies are based on *competition*, where the aim of advocates is to "win at any cost" rather than discover the truth or ensure the best outcome.

Increasingly, prisons are being privatized, so that greed is more nakedly involved in the institution. If it were not so profitable to owning-class forces to use the very cheap labor of prisoners, there would be more motivation to notice that the cost of keeping a person in prison for a year (paid for by the society) is substantially more than the typical salary of a social worker. Thus the money that could be used for fundamental change of the people caught in the prison system, if social workers understood the discharge process and the resulting elimination of patterns, would be available in the costs of keeping prisoners imprisoned.

It is not only the prisoners who are damaged by this institution. Its agents—prison guards, police officers, judges, lawyers, who are mostly men—are dehumanized by being put into these roles.

This institution, like the armed services, has a pervasive influence in society. It is a key factor in perpetuating the myths that men are violent and that there are "good" people and "bad" people. It stands behind the entrenched but wrong notion that punishment and threats are "good" ways to deal with certain kinds of distressed behaviors. (Young children, for example, are often told that if they behave in one way they will be taken to a "mental health" institution, or if they behave in another way they will be taken to prison.) The legal system, prisons, and police act as a threat to "keep everyone in line." Police forces have been extensively used for control of social movements under pretext of "security." Every time the working class mobilizes for defense of its interests and tries to build a strong labor movement, bargain collectively, and strike, the police have been used as an easily available force to defeat such organizing efforts and to intensify the exploitation of the workers.

GOALS
Replace criminal courts, police, and prisons with an intelligent way of handling violent patterns and any dangers they pose to other people in the world.

STRATEGIES

a) Act on the following principles and introduce them into public discussion and policy:

• "Every single human being, at every moment of the past, if the entire situation is taken into account, has always done the very best that he or she could do and so deserves neither blame nor reproach from anyone, including self. This, in particular, is true of you."

• Since every person has always done the very best that he or she could do at every moment of the past, blame or guilt or shame is unjustified in any circumstances and is harmful rather than useful in its effect upon anyone.

• Punishment, as punishment, always adds to the likelihood of irrational behavior instead of serving to prevent it or reduce its likelihood. Only discharge and re-evaluation free people to be rational in the areas where they have been irrational or destructive in the past.

• Imprisonment or isolation as punishment tends to make the misbehavior of any individual worse instead of better.

• Imprisonment or isolation to protect people from being harmed by the operation of destructive patterns attached to and operating on a person may be rational and justifiable temporarily, *but only as an emergency measure.* A better permanent solution must be found to end the emergency.

• Any person isolated or imprisoned in order to protect others from the pattern dominating that person is entitled to effective counseling, counseling which will eventually achieve the freedom of the person from the pattern.[16]

---

[16] "Counseling" refers to Re-evaluation Counseling, a well-defined-by-now practice of taking turns listening and allowing and assisting "discharge," which has the effect upon participants of becoming intelligent where they had previously been confused.

24

• No person nor institution operating on any level or under any circumstances has any "right" to deprive another person of life, *ever.*

• A deeply distressed person can be expected to (and can be skillfully required to) participate in the discharge, re-evaluation, and re-emergence that will restore the person to full human functioning and make him or her a safe companion for other people.

• Regardless of appearances or behavior, the most severely patterned, misfunctioning, and "dangerous" person retains his or her complete inherent humanness, goodness, and value even though these qualities may be obscured and seem to be made inoperative by the operation of the pattern. Such a person, however much his or her goodness is concealed and seemingly made inoperative by distress patterns, is nevertheless ultimately reachable with enough decisive counseling and, once reached, will eagerly cooperate in his or her own recovery of humanness.

• Recovery of a person's humanness will progress more quickly if strong, clear expectations of excellent functioning are supportively projected upon the person. These shall include the expectation that the person will not only discharge but will also decide to act, and act, on his or her full human power in order to restore full human functioning to himself or herself and restore full safety to other people in his or her environment.

• Each man needs to be cared for and thought about as an individual, and society must be required to pay this kind of attention to all men and to every man.

b) Publicize widely full information about the prison system and its basically irrational, oppressive nature. Encourage organization of people concerned about the treatment of prisoners; have them keep in contact with prisoners, guards, social workers, and the prison bureaucracy. Challenge the myth that "most" prisoners are violent and thus must be confined for the protection of the general population. Re-deploy resources to provide counseling in prisons to effectively help people deal with their distresses. Where prisons are temporarily unavoidable, they should be supervised and reviewed for humanness and for treating prisoners with fundamental respect.

c) Publicly expose, challenge, and organize against the open use of violence against males, beginning in childhood and continuing during adult life. Expose the connection between childhood abuse and adult patterns of violence. Police brutality, harassment, suppression of political dissent, and torture, particularly of men from oppressed groups, need to be targeted and exposed. Organize to bring political pressure to eliminate these behaviors.

d) Support existing alternatives to prisons, including dispute resolution/mediation, restorative justice (which brings together victims and perpetrators), and alternative sentencing to community service.

C. The Workplace Exploitation of Men as Workers

Work is inherently a very positive thing for all humans, including men. Basically, it consists of improving the environment that we function in so that it is supportive to our well-being and to our enjoyment, and to the onward-upward trend[17] of the humans who do the work.

> *Unlittered woods, an unpolluted stream,*
> *A fresh-swept hearth, one's body showered clean,*
> *Soil tilled with care, tools in their proper place*
> *Tell the real nature of our human race.*
>
> from "The Uses of Beauty and Order"

---

[17] "Upward trend" refers to tending toward order, toward meaning, toward integration, toward growth, toward intelligence and awareness, and toward independence.

Oppression entered the field of work with the beginning of class societies (the slave owner-slave societies to begin with, the noble-serf [feudal] societies later, and the owning class-middle class-wage worker society in the present epoch). These class societies introduced exploitation and misery and degradation into the operation of work, because the motivation of oppression is not for the general good except incidentally, but for the profit of a small section of the population. Oppression spoils and distorts the constructive nature of work. Work's inherent constructive nature can only be restored with the changing of society to end the oppression, which has, in a class society, been allowed to dominate and damage the rational function of work.

The principal channel for the financial exploitation of the working-class-majority-component of any society is exactly the overwork of its members. The overwhelming share of the surplus value extracted by the society for transfer to the owning class comes from the intense *overwork* of the working class, and the greatest intensity of this, at least as applied to "wage work," falls upon the male workers.

The dirtiest, most damaging, most dangerous, and most exhausting "paid" jobs and the unhealthiest working conditions have always tended to be loaded on men. Working with explosives, toxic chemicals, unsafe machinery, in bad weather, and when injured—all of these are standard situations for many, many men world-wide. (Ninety-seven percent of all fatal industrial accidents in the United Kingdom happen to men.) Many other men labor under the burden of dull, meaningless work. Nearly all men have to take what work they can get, often for long hours for very low pay.

Men work too hard and too long. Men in all workplaces are expected to perform unreasonable jobs within unreasonable limits, with few if any resources, human or otherwise. Even middle-class men, supposedly with easier jobs, are routinely expected to work brutally long hours, "exempt" from any overtime pay at all, because they are considered "professionals." Often the actual conditions for these middle-class "professionals" amount to working for very long hours and for very low pay.

Men work in competition with other men, alone, and often in isolation, so that there is no cooperation or room to call for help when things get hard. Men are often set up to compete for a central role or position in whatever space they're in. This competition gets heightened when resources seem particularly scarce, for example, when layoffs are threatened, or when disadvantaged groups compete with themselves or each other for room within the system.

The exploiters of men as workers tend primarily to *be* men. Men are often bribed with higher pay and prestige to take on the job of being exploiters.

Men are treated as expendable: "If you can't handle the job, there's lots of unemployed." Unemployment is systematically manipulated to create a surplus labor pool, reduce wages, discourage worker organizing, and encourage competition for jobs.

Men are seen as having no value except to work or to make a profit for someone else. They are encouraged to have as their goal making more money and buying "more" or "better" things. They are denigrated if they are not part of this competitive purchasing system, even if the system does not allow them to be a part of it because of their race, age, class position, or disability.

Overwork and insecurity are used to prevent access to emotional discharge, closeness, active involvement in parenting, and organizing to change things. Dependence of families' well-being on men's income coerces men into accepting bad conditions and overwork. Men's love of their families is thus turned against them.

Some effects on men's lives of the institutions of the workplace are:

• Men become tired, stupefied, bitter, cynical, unable to work supportively with other people;

• Men become exhausted, physically damaged, and their health suffers;

• Men are left without strength, leisure, or time for family, closeness, creativity, and play;

• Men often feel on edge, without security, as if they have no value other than what they can produce;

• Men are led to take pride in and defend their patterns of enduring mistreatment and overwork;

• Men are corrupted by the system into working its will (rather than their own).

The workplace as an institution also has great impact on the lives of those *excluded* from it, those who are unemployed. For some men, particularly men of color, this can mean whole communities. Large numbers of black men are chronically unemployed in the United States. Under the current economic system, many have little chance for more than occasional employment throughout their lives. In the United Kingdom there is an underclass of young men who have left school and never expect to be able to work. Many other oppressed groups are also vulnerable to being excluded from the world of paid work, such as people with disabilities and older men. Some of the effects of unemployment on men are:

• Unemployed men often experience a feeling of worthlessness that can lead to suicide, addictions, etc.;

• Unemployed men are denied the opportunity and rewards of a productive life;

• Unemployed men tend to identify themselves with the labels that society assigns them ("lazy good-for-nothings") and the patterns that they bear as the result of their mistreatment;

• Unemployed men's family connections are often strained and broken as a result of the unmet social expectation that they will financially support their families.

GOALS

Make safe, meaningful work available to all men. To do this completely will require eliminating the class society based on exploitation and profit-making, and replacing it with an economic system based on intelligence, closeness, caring, and the natural joy of work.

STRATEGIES

a) Challenge the authority and policies of the class society's oppressive organizations (corporations, political action groups, and government agencies) that carry out their oppression in a visible, public way. This activity will be a necessary step toward establishing an economic system capable of sustaining meaningful and human work for all.

b) Build strong labor union movements everywhere, building them from the bottom up, guaranteeing control of them by their members (not by employer agencies or criminal gangs that are really serving the interests of the owning class), with maximum involvement of ordinary workers. Labor unions must advance new policies which require compensation for all labor based on its true value to society, and not just on profit-making.

c) Tackle overall the elimination of the conditioned greed for money, not only in the owning classes of the society, but where it has systematically been conditioned onto all the other classes. Speak out for the reduction of time spent at work, for "part-time work," for more holidays, job security, and income security for both the employed and the unemployed, for structures that allow employees to communicate with each other, and so on. In all places, workplaces or elsewhere, men should spearhead the call to work cooperatively, for the good of all, instead of competitively for individual "gain."

Eliminate any current attitudes that men are required to overwork in order to secure basic food, water, and shelter. Eliminate any oppressive programs that give the appearance that men are required to destroy the environment in order to survive. ("If we don't kill off all the whales, if we don't cut down all the trees, then we won't have any jobs.")

D. The Sex Industries

Closeness to other humans is an inherent need for all humans. This closeness is involved with the subtle complexities of our existence, with the rational interaction of one intelligence with another. Sexual interaction guided by informed intelligence can be an elegant part of that closeness, but closeness need not involve sex, or sexual feelings, to be complete, rational, enjoyable, and a positive activity. Sex without closeness can be imagined in desperate situations, but closeness does not require sex for completeness, and closeness can be very complete and satisfactory without it.

Humans come equipped with sexual instincts, which in our earlier evolution were undoubtedly necessary to the continuation of our species, but which, like our other instincts, can come (and in the absence of patterns have come) under the control of our intelligence. There is no "human" need for sex (as distinct from our species' need for procreation).

Most (perhaps all) of our existing cultures (which are already contaminated with patterns) treat nearly all closeness between genders as being available *only* through sex, rather than through deep emotional connection, through intelligence, through camaraderie, and

31

through fun. In these patterned cultures, there is a contaminated confusion between closeness and sex, and many men have been left with a rigid attitude that "closeness is available only through sex." This channels the need for human contact and connection into what comes to feel like a need for sex in order to have closeness. This approach usually leads to a backlog of desperate loneliness, a frozen preoccupation with sex, and lives dominated by sexual compulsions and inhibitions.

All such patterned sexual compulsions and inhibitions can be discharged, and discharged completely, through enough effective counseling. Some of the very good work that has been done in Re-evaluation Counseling has been done under the direction "to address and discharge on every memory that has any kind of connection with sex at all, and discharge it thoroughly."

Children are naturally interested in sex, as they are in all human functioning. This interest is, however, often contaminated by adult-imposed secrecy, condemnation, and shame. It is nearly impossible for children to receive access to information about sex separate from the distresses of adults. In many cultures and religions, sex is considered inappropriate to talk about and regarded as "a necessary evil."

The mishandling of information about sex and leaving children's education about it to furtive gossip between their peers amounts to abandoning boys as they try to figure out an area that they have already concluded is of paramount importance to "being a man."

Many men have other experiences as boys that compound distress about sex, including sexual abuse. Men rarely have been helped to talk and discharge about these experiences so that they can become more rational as they grow older. As a result, some of these men who were originally abused as boys feel compelled to act out upon others the sexual distresses that were originally perpetrated upon them. These experiences of sexual distress tend to make all relationships difficult for men.

The substantial backlog of distress about sex, accumulated from childhood, has formed the basis for a huge world-wide market for sexual materials. This market is driven by men's preoccupation with sex, which is also an unaware attempt to escape the loneliness and isolation of men's oppression. Participation in these activities, however, actually does nothing to relieve the loneliness but instead adds another layer of shame and despair. The sex industry includes prostitution, strip joints, pornographic movies and magazines, World Wide Web sites, phone sex, and any other profit-making businesses based on selling something intended to restimulate distress recordings that include sexual feelings. Other related industries, like entertainment and advertising, also capitalize on men's preoccupation with sex as a means to sell their products. In our society, sexual interest is used to manipulate men's distress rather than to inform them.

The sex industries are harmful to men in a number of ways. These include the following:

• Perhaps the worst effect is the shame and self-disgust that many men are loaded with. They internalize the message that they are to "blame" for their frozen preoccupation with sex. In fact, this preoccupation is reinforced by society and based on hurtful experiences they endured that they were in no position to prevent or avoid.

• There is a transfer of huge sums of money from the customers to the owners of the sex industries. Some estimate that the pornography industries are more lucrative than all of the Hollywood enterprises.

• The sex industries serve as a diversion from liberation and other rational activities, including real closeness.

• The sex industries harm men's and women's relationships with each other. Often patterned attitudes (portraying women as "sex objects") have been installed by the distress in the culture to replace the natural response of relaxed affection between men and women. These tense preoccupations come up around women, and the culture has attached shame to this. All people sense intuitively that involvement with the various phases of the sex industries is not rational. The sex industries are dehumanizing to both men and women.

• Preoccupation with sexual tension can become addictive, just as any other distress can become addictive, and can ruin people's lives if it is not discharged.

A MAN NEED NOT REMAIN PREOCCUPIED WITH SUCH AN ADDICTION. PERSISTENT COUNSELING CAN LEAVE ONE PERMANENTLY RELAXED AND AT EASE IN THE WHOLE AREA.

GOALS

Expose the pornography "industry" and other "sex industries" as totally harmful to men. Eliminate pornography and other uses of sex to manipulate men's emotions on the basis that they are destructive to both men's and women's lives. In particular, prevent any further installation of patterns (including addictive patterns) through any irrational treatment of women and through any embarrassment, shame, and humiliation imposed on males around sex.

STRATEGIES

a) Information about sex can be presented without tension or embarrassment, but simply as a part of living that can be understood in its entirety by anybody and everyone. Organize people in schools, in families, and in special meetings, to remove all mystery and embarrassment from the realities of sex and sexual practice.

Encourage people to tell their own sexual histories, starting with the earliest memory connected with sex *in any way at all*.

b) Never withhold real closeness from any male, particularly not on the basis that it is not manly to need to be close. Challenge all social forms that treat boys as not needing human closeness, or that offer sex as "an escape" from their isolation as males. Establish support groups for men to free themselves from sexual addictions and to assist them in establishing close, human relationships with other men and with women. Promote openness and honesty about sex. Assist people to think about when and with whom a sexual relationship may, can, and should be started.

c) Assist the men who are victims of the sex industries to recognize the harmful nature of these industries and the harmful impact on their lives. Create the conditions necessary for the men (and women) who are victims of the sex industries to tell the real stories of their lives. Establish support groups for men addicted to pornography, phone sex, etc., and provide counseling resource to assist men to break free of these addictions and reclaim full lives.

d) Expose the motives of greed and profiteering that fuel the sex industries.

E. The Alcohol, Tobacco, Pharmaceutical, and Illegal Drug Industries

Men are the primary victims of the powerful alcohol, tobacco, and drug industries. This victimization is more and more extended to women as the society "matures" to the point of near collapse. However, men are "expected" to be the principal participants in and the principal victims of drug and alcohol abuse. This abuse of men is offered as a way of "assuaging" the injuries and ill health that are part of men's lives and are expected by them as a matter of course. In many countries, the standard means of "recovering" from the intense overwork of men's jobs is to "stop in the tavern" on the way home.

The role and goal of the multi-national alcohol industry is to normalize use of alcohol in every part of society. Alcohol becomes identified with a wide range of images that men are trained to view as positive, including sex, sports, success, and physical beauty. All this conditioning feeds a denial at the societal level that alcohol is a drug at all or that it is one of the more deadly and costly drugs in all societies. The entire society is manipulated into accepting alcohol's presence and importance in men's lives, and, in the United States since "Prohibition," is oriented toward blaming the drinking man, rather than the drink, for the problems men's drinking causes for them and for those around them.

Alcohol use also undergirds many other problems in the society, and its role in them often goes unrecognized. These problems include domestic violence, rape, homicide, suicide, transmission of sexually-transmitted diseases, drownings, falls, motor vehicle crashes, and workplace injuries. Alcohol also feeds the persistent economic under-development of poor communities and countries, where a history of encouraging alcohol outlets and industries leaves a legacy that is inhospitable to the development of other sources of income.

The global tobacco industry markets the most addictive drug known to humanity with virtual impunity across the globe. Despite clear proofs that the industry has known for years how addictive and deadly the drug it markets is, it has successfully bought off political leaders in country after country and has found myriad ways to press its products and logos upon the public. Because tobacco tends to kill its users near the end of their "productive" lives, it has served oppressive societies well. A strong stand needs to be taken against this "killing-off" of men (and increasingly, women) now that the dangers of tobacco use are well known.

The illegal drug industry functions in many inner-city and minority communities in the United States as the primary means of employment and economic support. Forces in the oppressive society such as the Central Intelligence Agency have encouraged and at least tacitly supported the illegal domestic drug trade, at the same time that other oppressive forces have used it as a means of controlling minority populations in the United States and interfering in the internal affairs of other nations. To justify oppressive drug wars, myths have been propounded regarding the supposed dominance of young black and Latino males among drug users in the United States. In fact, the majority of drug users are white men, while black and Latino men are greatly over-represented among those who suffer the repressive consequences of the most recent "drug war."

What is labeled a "good drug" or a "bad drug" in the society is more often determined for social rather than for medical reasons. The prescription drug industry is the primary purveyor of the drugs that the society has labeled as "good." Although some prescription drugs do bring benefits to humans, the organization of the industry for profit distorts its ability to serve the health of the public and subjects it to enormous pressure to continue to define new clinical "conditions" that require its newest drugs. Although in this era, women have been the primary targets of the new classes of psychoactive drugs, drugs such as Ritalin, Viagra, and anti-depressants are pressed upon men and boys as well. If men cannot be seduced by drugs, they are prescribed them.

That boys in the United States are currently, in large numbers, being given Ritalin to control behavior (behavior that is the result of being mistreated as boys during this period of societal collapse) marks the spread of the oppressive "mental health" organization to a new "target market." This oppressive activity directed at boys is creating a whole new generation of men who will be easier to oppress and addict to other drugs later in life because of early damage to their central nervous systems by Ritalin and other drugs, as well as early damage to their sense of their own power by being forced to take drugs against their will.

Tobacco, alcohol, mood- and mind-altering drugs, and psychoactive drugs, whether legal or illegal, interfere with the process of discharge and re-evaluation. They also function to keep men distracted and unable to organize to remove the causes of their unhappiness, which lie in the irrational organization of the society to support the profit-making of the few at the expense of the many.

Men today have been systematically denied access to the discharge process. There is a direct relationship between the use of drugs and alcohol and suppression of the discharge process. Whenever society doesn't want men to feel something, it will tend to drug them so that they won't feel it. Multi-national drug corporations addict young males to these substances on the false basis that they will provide "relaxation," "enjoyment," and "relief from stress." In reality, the use of these products destroys bodies and minds and creates an environment in which destructive and self-destructive behaviors thrive. Meanwhile, the real sources of stress go unchallenged. These include loneliness, dangerous or unsatisfying work conditions, unemployment or underemployment, and the deeply inhibited ability to discharge and re-evaluate.

By discharging the distress recordings that underlie the addiction, it is possible to eliminate any form of addiction that keeps people from being able to change their lives the way they want to.

GOALS

Eliminate any form of profit-making in relation to the supply of alcohol, tobacco, or other drugs. Make public the information that any addiction can be fully recovered from and assist men to do so. Organize humans to end the targeting of men by alcohol, tobacco, and other drug industries. Expose the special extra oppression inflicted on men of color and communities of color by their being falsely blamed as the active agents for spreading drug use.

STRATEGIES

a) Organize humans everywhere to remove profit from the production and sale of drugs, and to remove the unwanted presence of these drug industries from people's lives. Promote alternative forms of economic development that don't rest on the alcohol and drug industries. Educate the public about the social movements throughout history that have successfully motivated people to stop using drugs and to confront the oppressive forces that produce and market them.

b) Furnish counseling assistance to men to recover fully from all addictions, by teaching Re-evaluation Counseling and setting up RC support groups widely, focusing on discharging the distress recordings that underlie addictions. Promote complete integration of the discharge process into the daily practice of men, so that they may discharge both physical and emotional distresses, as part of ending the efforts of the oppressive society to replace men's bad feelings (produced by oppression and mistreatment) with the numbness produced by drugs. Finally, we need to challenge the real sources of stress: loneliness, dangerous or unsatisfying work conditions, unemployment or underemployment, and the deeply inhibited ability to discharge and re-evaluate.

c) Expose the racism and classism behind these industries, and the mechanism of targeting communities of people of color and communities of poor, working-class people.

F. The Sports Industries

Sports in themselves can serve many beneficial, rational functions. They can encourage men (and women) to use their bodies in powerful, dynamic, vibrant ways. They can provide "safe" opportunities to challenge one's restimulation around abilities and perceived limitations, and to act on the basis of power. They give us opportunities to see men being courageous and inspiring. They can be an attractive, safe channel for exercise and the development of skills, an environment for making new friends, and a way to express a sense of community and cooperation.

However, sports have been saddled by the oppressive society with an intense burden of "competition," which tends to put every male in the position of being a potential antagonist to every other male. This situation has been exposed as a training ground for preparing young males for their roles of killing or being killed as soldiers in war and preparing males to participate in the class society (in which they are expected to compete with each other for economic survival and advancement).

The sports industries are directly exploitative of, and damaging to, the men who participate in them. They actively exploit men of color (especially black and Latino men in the United States) as profit-making devices for professional team owners and sports-equipment manufacturers. In addition, they create and support undisguised models of greed. They prey upon and manipulate the economic desperation of young males in lower-income communities, encouraging an irrational consumerism based on manipulated "loyalties" and symbols.

Sports are presented as "the way out" of poverty for many young males, ignoring the development of the complete person in deference to the athletic performance, taking the "best" and discarding the rest. Even the "chosen ones" are themselves discarded as soon as they no longer serve their function as audience-drawing athletes. The huge amount of money involved in major professional sports is used to justify men destroying their physical and emotional health.

In some countries the sports industries serve to perpetuate sectarianism and nationalism (Catholic versus Protestant, England versus Brazil, etc.), encouraging the use of sports as yet another arena for inter-group antagonisms to be acted out and maintained.

The sports industry also acts to drain off men's intelligence and to keep men muddled and confused, frustrated and passive. Men have a spontaneous desire for personal meaning, non-material-based success, and human satisfaction. Their efforts and strategies would certainly fuel social change of a profound character if encouraged and directed. Instead men's vigor and passion are drowned in pseudo-emotions and drained off in pseudo-emotional release, by being induced to identify with "our team," "our hero," and the violent expressions on behalf of "our" symbol against "their" symbol.

In addition to organized team activities, there are other "manly" recreational activities set up by the society to distract men from meaningful activity and distort men's relationships to each other and the world. Among these are gambling and recreational hunting.

GOALS

We need to transform organized sports from a greed- and profit-based activity centered around the false goal of "winning" against another human being, into an activity based on cooperation, overall human unity, mutual respect, and fun.

41

STRATEGIES

a) Teach and organize around the notion of sports as a means for men to challenge each other to grow in skill, to deepen and strengthen relationships across "differences," to keep "play" in their lives, and to encourage the care and enjoyment of their bodies. Clarify sports as an excellent channel for enjoyment of supportive striving, inspiration, and the mutual achievement of excellence. Encourage and incorporate discharge as a natural component of any sports activity.

b) Intelligently revise competition in the direction of men's being *of assistance* to each other. Transform or eliminate all sports activities which involve men brutalizing each other or themselves. Expose the connection between the ruthless competitive mentality presently encouraged by the sports industries and the preparation of young males to kill or be killed in war.

G. Schools

Schools originally developed to bring organizational support to students in their *learning*. At their best, they have brought together adults who are intelligent about helping people learn and young people who are still eager to learn. Schools can give students an opportunity to be together, learn from each other, acquire life skills, and widen their view of the world. For some young people in current societies, they are also a safe haven from harmful home and neighborhood circumstances.

Unfortunately, in our current situation they have become a primary means for socializing boys from a young age to accept without too much question the oppressed role assigned to a man and the oppressed role assigned to a worker in our society.

Schools, as institutions, play a very large role in fostering the oppression of men. They actively oppress males by encouraging competition instead of cooperation, by suppressing discharge, by dividing boys into the "good" and the "bad," by providing a distorted view of history, and by glorifying war and war heroes. By being irrelevant and meaningless to the lives of many young males, schools fail to nurture them as valuable members of the society.

Schools are likely boys' first exposure to government-sponsored institutionalized oppression. School teaches a boy to "act like a man." Schools induct boys into conforming to the oppressive society and all its oppressions. Young people are acclimated to scarcity of approval. They learn to conform to the school's notion of "what is good behavior," "what is bad behavior," "what is a girl," "what is a boy," "what happens to you when you don't do what is expected of you," etc.

Although military service and prisons are places where men are obviously scapegoated, mistreated, and abused, much of what happens there is set up by what happens to boys. Because young people are naturally eager to learn, eager to be active and playful, schools are usually poorly matched to young people's learning styles and levels of activity. Young people don't learn well when forced to sit at desks for long hours. Boys, who tend to have been less conditioned into passivity than many girls, are punished more under these learning conditions where passivity and timidity are rewarded. Boys unable to conform are often invalidated, criticized, blamed, and punished. This treatment deeply reinforces the message that boys are "bad." Schools in the United States categorize boys early into "troublemakers" and "good boys." Most boys are told that they are either "bad" because they are acting out of the rigid norm for a "good student," or "good" because they follow the rigid norm and "work." These attitudes become magnified by the racism usually practiced in schools. This harsh and invalidating treatment starts an alarmingly high number of African-American boys on a path toward prison or early death. Most suspensions and expulsions are of boys, giving them the message that society is "willing to give up on them."

The systematic intimidation combined with suppression of discharge really takes hold in the school atmosphere. Boys are pitted against boys in the classroom in competition for grades and class ranking, in strength contests, and in "organized" sports. On the schoolyard and on the way home younger or weaker boys are "bullied" by boys who were themselves previously bullied.

Self-worth is linked directly to achievement. Boys are divided into "winners" and "losers," and few boys "measure up." Throughout the school years, boys make up the majority of students at the bottom of the class in academic achievement. Boys are also disproportionately over-represented among those diagnosed as having "learning disabilities" and among those failing academically. The internalized feelings of lack of worth and stupidity attach onto boys' feelings that they are "bad," and many never recover from this image of themselves as being "dumb."

In the United States schools play a hurtful role in supporting and implementing the drugging of young boys with Ritalin and other psychiatric drugs, in response to behaviors that are the result of the schools' failure to accommodate to boys' needs.

It is also harmful to boys to spend large parts of their childhood and school experiences with few if any *male* teachers or *male* role models. The chronic low pay and low respect given to teachers still keeps most males from even considering a teaching career.

GOALS

Schools must be transformed into forces for liberation and vehicles for teaching basic democratic principles *and ways of caring deeply for one another,* in addition to furnishing an informed education. Schools need to make available to all students the tools for self-initiated, lifelong learning. Schools need to be transformed into institutions where boys are valued as boys and nurtured to be successful.

STRATEGIES

a) Boys should learn about justice, equity, and inclusion. They should be taught an accurate view of history, of how the world works, and how the world *should* work. They should learn about oppression and liberation. Their natural interest in fairness should be encouraged, and they should be equipped with the skills to stand up against injustice and oppression in all its forms.

b) Schools should be adapted to fit the needs of boys, rather than expecting boys to fit the current structures of schools. Specifically, schools need to be organized so that differences in learning styles are allowed for. Schools should support boys to learn through play and activity, and should develop instructional methods that enable *all* boys to be successful.

c) Schools need to actively support the discharge process for boys and girls alike. Schools should support and encourage the full range of human qualities for boys, outside all limiting gender roles. All students need to be taught an accurate view of the nature of males. Schools should encourage boys to tell their stories and let others know what their lives are truly like.

d) We need to eliminate the present categorization of boys as either "troublemakers" or "good boys" so that they can see their goodness as young men, apart from their ability to "do something" or "follow instructions." We need parents and teachers who can think well enough about boys to not do this *and* care for them so that they can grow up knowing that it is possible for people to care for and think well of each other. Boys should be validated and fully supported to know their own goodness. Because boys need a community of support, parents should be invited to participate in every part of children's education.

e) Competition in schools should be eliminated, enabling educators to rely on eliciting students' natural curiosity for motivation in learning. All classification of students into "smart and dumb" or "good and bad" must be replaced by *success* for each and every student. Schools should never give up on any student.

f) All categories of school employees, including teachers, should be approximately fifty percent men in number, to provide good role models and a personal understanding of men's issues. Teachers should be adequately compensated for doing some of the most important work that is done in the society. Teachers should be trained to handle and give assistance to boys with the distress patterns that society frequently installs on boys and then blames and punishes them for, such as being violent, loud, cynical, arrogant, "cool" and disinterested, etc. All punishment should be eliminated, including punishment for violence and mistreatment among boys. It should be replaced with assistance in discharging distresses that lead to boys' harming others and themselves.

g) Schools should refuse to participate in the drugging of students and educate parents about the harmful effects of psychoactive medications. Eliminate "hazing" and all "games" or rituals designed to "test" masculinity or manhood. End bullying.

H. Religions

Throughout history people have sought to find meaning in their lives, and to understand reality and intelligence as distinct from pseudo-reality and distress.[18] Often religions began as attempts to help people find this meaning. The theologies of various religions have had many positive ideas (e.g., "love thy neighbor," "repair the world"). Religious institutions have made attempts to build communities of people, to provide people with a place to stand up for what they believe in, and to provide structures to fight against poverty and for human liberation. Unfortunately, religious institutions also have been largely co-opted by *class* systems to separate people from one another and to provide yet another means of social control.

Many religions throughout history have caused separations between people, have brought about bloody "holy" wars, "we" and "they" separations, "our God" and "their God" separations, martyrs of all sorts, suicides, and other irrational behaviors. Current examples surround us (e.g., Ireland, Yugoslavia, the Middle East). Men are required to kill and be killed in the name of some religions. Many religions encourage confusion around sex and insist on the invalidating idea of "sin." Some religions encourage some men to refrain from sexual relations altogether and from building families. Some religions encourage the oppression of Gay people and the sexist oppression of females. All people are in some ways victims of religious institutions, but males are often the main victims. Circumcision is only one of many "religious" ideas for imposing pain and terror on a very young male child.

---

[18] "Pseudo-reality" refers to a false picture of reality which is imposed upon us as a substitute for reality. It is a distortion of reality presented to us by oppression, by other people's patterns, by our own patterns, by misinformation, and by the societies in which we live.

Religions are steeped in rigid notions of what people are like and the roles that men are "expected" to play. Often these rigid notions are founded in the idea, promoted by almost all organized religions, that God is a male—this idea provides the bedrock for patriarchy within religious institutions and within the family. Religions provide an irrational, rigid model of what a family "should" be like. Men are cast as patriarchs and as "in charge of the family," while women are made to be subservient, which robs men of their full humanness and installs sexist oppression. Religions interfere with men's needs to be close to many people in their lives, not restricted just to an often "thin" relationship with one's partner in marriage.

Religions discourage people from doing their own thinking by providing a set of beliefs for people to adopt without thinking. Religions are also a large factor in forcing men to adopt pretense. Religions cause men to hide things that they do and to think that feelings they have been made to feel are "socially unacceptable."

Often religions legitimize suffering and cause it to be sought out because "martyred" lives are considered virtuous. For example, the Protestant work ethic encourages men to see value only through their work and to exhaust themselves at work.

Religions are *not wholly* committed in a negative way. The negative *forces within the religions are often being combatted by progressive forces*, which are also within the religions, seeking to take a pro-people direction. Religions can be places where the struggles between attempts to be intelligent and attempts to insist on continuing unintelligence can be dealt with, sometimes encouragingly.

GOALS

We need to issue a call for a basic agreement among all "religious" people in every religious organization to put themselves forward as a force for intelligent activity, for the liberation of all people, and for permanently ending all armed conflict.

STRATEGIES

a) Organize campaigns to demand that all religions declare themselves against armed conflict by *any group* against *any group*. Expose the function of religion in furnishing a cover for exploitation and warmongering with the excuse of religious differences. Call for an end to the use of religion and religious structures (such as the "religious right" in the United States) as a cover for any anti-democratic activity or as supports for any oppression and exploitation of human beings.

b) End any rigid oppressive models of "males" promulgated through organized religions. Consider acceptance of women priests and other religious leaders as rational models. Eliminate the concept of "sin." Eliminate condemnation of sex by organized religions, including condemnation of boyhood sexuality by religious authorities. Insist on a rational attitude toward sex in religious instruction of priests and religious leaders. End any mutilation of children for religious purposes.

c) Call for a world-wide meeting of religious leaders in order to address each of these proposals.

I. The Family

Mothers and fathers naturally love their male children. Still, from birth, boys in our present societies have been treated differently than girls. The family is the first place the role-definition of "what it means to be a man" is taught and enforced, the first place most boys receive a model of what they are and aren't supposed to grow up to be like. From the very beginning, boys are held and talked to less than girls, under the false assumption that being a man means that boys must be able to handle things "on their own" and must not complain. As they have grown older, boys have been pushed out to handle the world by themselves. Within the family, boys have often been isolated, have often had violence perpetrated upon them, and have been encouraged to isolate and hurt others for showing any emotion, zest, or curiosity. They have even been typically harshly condemned for standing up for themselves.

In the present societies, parents usually "intentionally" prepare their boys to "fit in." Unfortunately this means preparing them to become perpetrators of oppression toward women and "bullies" or "victims" of other men. The family installs patterns of self-abuse and of addictive numbing-out that make it possible for men to go to war, endure overwork, and not have satisfying lives nor close relationships with others.

Boys must not be abandoned. They need parents close to them, providing nurture, information, guidance, companionship, and cherishing. They need parents who are actively involved in their lives from birth until maturity at least. Boys need to be truly appreciated just for their existence, independent of what they might do for someone else and independent of their families' dreams for them.

Many cultures assume that fathers will not be closely involved with their children. In most "First World" societies, where men are rewarded for overwork and where productivity is valued over humanness, fathers are seen primarily as the providers, who sacrifice for the family unit rather than being involved supportively in their children's lives. This is hard on both fathers and children, depriving them of closeness with one another.

GOALS
Transform the family into a functioning unit that provides full support for boys.

STRATEGIES

a) Eliminate the ways that parents are kept on the edge economically, as well as exhausted physically, so that they, instead, have the optimum chance and time to think about their children. Provide families with the resources and support, the information and the models, to let male children become adults with their confidence and self-respect intact. Provide all children with a community of adults to think about them and their families and to intervene with assistance when necessary.

b) Encourage parents to hold and stay close to their male children, and to cherish their male children for who they are, rather than for what they do. Encourage parents to commit themselves to never isolate or hit their male children.

c) Eliminate any economic or social structure that keeps men from being actively engaged in parenting. Make paid paternity leave from work a right everywhere, and, where it already exists as a right, encourage men to use it. Provide all fathers, whatever their circumstances, with counseling and support to reclaim their inherent desire to have real relationships with their children, including their sons. Organize support groups for fathers to meet, communicate, and discharge.

These nine institutions and their supporting structures are the forces that principally stand behind and direct the extraction of the spoils of the class society. These are the structures that men and their allies must courageously outmaneuver, take apart, and replace with a decent society.[19]

---

[19] "Allies" refers to people who are supportive of the good functioning and successful re-emergence of other people. Allies encourage the people to whom they are allies, helping them discharge the distresses that are getting in their way, and assisting them towards functioning well in their daily lives.

OTHER SOCIETAL ASPECTS
OF MEN'S OPPRESSION

Homophobia and Gay Oppression

All humans have a deep need for closeness with other humans, regardless of gender.

Homophobia is "the fear of being close to someone of the same gender as oneself." Fear of closeness between men is enforced with viciousness and violence in most cultures and on a world-wide scale. It adds violence and prejudice in nearly every situation. In many societies, men are raised to compete viciously with other men, to scorn men who are different from the culturally-enforced norm, and to seek and accept closeness exclusively with women. This socially enforced fear of closeness between men provides a common basis for the attitudes that allow men to kill each other in wars, to engage in suicidal behaviors to "prove" their masculinity, and to terrorize women, men, and children whom they perceive to be weaker than themselves.

The terrorizing and scapegoating of some men by other men has been a critical part of the oppression of men. It sets up examples of what will happen should one resist oppression and step out of the "normal" role of "being male."

Gay oppression is the systematic mistreatment of people who identify as Gay, Lesbian, or bisexual. As well as having a cruel and devastating effect on the targeted groups, Gay oppression is used to terrorize all men into conformity to oppressive male roles.

Sexual relations between people of the same gender, and in particular between males, are treated with horror and disgust and terror in most cultures. *None of this is justified.* It is perfectly possible in every species of living creatures for individuals of the same gender to participate in sexual activity together and, in the case of humans, for distress recordings to be installed. These recordings tend to compel the individuals to persist in the sexual activity because of the strange feelings left from the experience. The recordings will often also include positive feelings of sexual desire and excitement, affection, and admiration, as well as physical closeness. The individuals carrying these distress recordings can then experience powerful attractions and compulsions toward participation in sex with people of the same gender. These attractions or compulsions will often seem to the participants to completely replace the instinctive attraction between different sexes typically regarded by the culture as "normal." Persistent use of Re-evaluation Counseling with a wide variety of clients has led to the conclusion that a person who carries a Gay pattern does so only as a result of distress recordings being installed in this way.

Freeing individuals from these patterns is perfectly possible and can be accomplished, but the extreme repression turned on individuals and organized in the cultures often makes this a difficult task. Being condemned, argued with, scolded, and rejected simply reinforces any patterned rigidities, confuses the rest of the population, and inhibits the discharge necessary for a person to freely give up participation in such a pattern (or, indeed, any pattern). Gay people in RC are not asked to commit themselves to give up a Gay life, but it has produced much discharge and movement out of distress to ask them to arrange sessions with each other, or with trusted allies, based on assuming that "it may be true" that Gayness is dependent on the installation of distress recordings. Since the entire subject is, at present, covered with distress in the present cultures, a warm and reasonable attitude by the counselor can make it possible for the *client* to cooperate enough and discharge enough that he (or she) can decide for himself (or herself) out of his (or her) own experience in counseling what he (or she) desires for himself (or herself) and his (or her) relationships.

GOALS

We seek to eliminate homophobia and Gay oppression. We seek to challenge them both at every turn. We seek to expose the origins of homosexuality and Gay oppression and assist people to discharge them.

STRATEGIES

a) Create and encourage opportunities for males to be close and allied with one another from the earliest age. Celebrate and encourage men's closeness with each other. Appreciate Gay men for modeling closeness between men and for prioritizing men's relationships with each other. In an era when in many Western cultures Gay oppression and homophobia have viciously interfered with men's ability to be close to each other, it has been for the most part Gay men who continue to show that such closeness is possible. However, this closeness has no inherent relationship to sex or to being Gay and is the birthright of every man.

b) Condemn any oppression of Gay people and, in particular, of Gay men. Expose the damaging effects of Gay oppression on Gay people, and on all human beings. Show how it is to the advantage of all humans to end Gay oppression. Express clearly that the RC Communities are thoroughly and completely committed against any oppression of Gay people and, in particular, against any oppression of Gay men.

c) Create an atmosphere of complete respect for Gay people, take an unwavering stand against the oppression of Gay people, and hold out to Gay people that it is possible to discharge all distresses related to sex, closeness, relationships with people of both genders, and sexual identities, and to make completely intelligent decisions regarding all aspects of their lives.

d) As a trusted ally, offer a Gay person the opportunity to arrange sessions with you where he may experiment with assuming that "it may be true" that Gayness is dependent on the installation of distress recordings. At the same time, take the position that it is *the client* who can and should decide for himself, out of his own experiences in counseling, what he desires for himself and his relationships.

Consumerism

Work *could be* the shared effort to produce and provide the goods and services needed by society to meet the needs of its members. Instead, work in most present societies is organized to maximize the accumulation of wealth by a small number of people using the labor of the vast majority in exchange for as little in wages as the class society can enforce. This means that the organizing principle of the work of the society is not what is required to meet the needs of the population as a whole, but instead, what can bring the most profit to the owning class of the society.

The modern markets of owning-class (capitalist) societies are organized around such phenomena as "consumerism" and "materialism" and the addictions to "toys" and to "keeping up with the Joneses." This consumerism is seen most clearly to date in the "First World" countries, but it is being exported world-wide. This consumerism is designed to create a market that can be manipulated to handle the kind of production that is most "profitable to produce." One result of this is that tremendous amounts of our resource and creativity are poured into strategizing about "what people will buy," thinking of how to make them "want to buy" products, to "spend money."

Buying things to make us "feel better" is encouraged as yet another way to channel men's hurts around not having their real needs met. The things men buy don't often actually make them feel better in any lasting way because what they really need is to discharge the hurts and make changes in their lives so that real needs are met. The addiction to buying things to try to make men "feel better" makes them spend more money and need to work harder or longer. This approach is harmful to men and is a vicious cycle. This attitude reinforces the various other ways men are pulled to overwork.

This requirement of "profitability" means that the production of goods and services is based on what the people with money will pay for, not what people in the society need. This means that much-needed work cannot be funded and people wanting work cannot be employed. At the same time lots of people are suffering from overwork.

Governments collect funds through taxation which they can spend independent of profit, but the people who make up the policies for the governments are typically dependent on the financial support of the people with the most money. So these people's interests are disproportionately represented. There is therefore no guarantee that money will really be spent for what people really need.

GOAL

Completely transform society from one based on profit via the exploitation of human beings to one based on caring and cooperative work to meet human needs.

STRATEGIES

Organize on every level to end every oppression and replace the present economic system. Organize people to discharge all recordings of greed. Create alternative institutions aimed at organizing and employing people to meet real human needs, funded in new and creative ways that prevent the interference of greed. For example, raise money to pay people to rebuild their own neighborhoods.

Men's Health

At present, as noted above, a variety of social factors lead men, in general, to die at younger ages than women do. Traditionally men have been deeply conditioned not to take care of their health, and men have a substantially higher rate of suicide than women in nearly all countries. In addition, men's internalized oppression often leads to self-destructive behavior. When these statistics are publicized, usually at least some men begin to take more of an interest in health and health care, and in why it might have been difficult for men to care about their health.

GOAL

See that excellent health care is available to all men and eliminate all conditions in society that lead to men dying young.

STRATEGIES

a) Use statistics on men's health as a way of opening up discussions about men's oppression and liberation. Catch men's attention by asking questions about their health. Educate health service providers about the reality of men's lives and men's oppression.

b) Identify and eliminate every social factor that shortens men's life expectancies, including poverty, overwork, violence, war, isolation, and lack of access to discharge. Offer every man the possibility of a long, relaxed, close, and productive life. Ensure that it will never again be acceptable in society that men die young.

Men as Allies to Young People

Men (and women) all inherently love to have close contact with infants and with children of all ages. Anyone of either gender is capable of being completely competent to play a positive role in the life of any young person. The usual social expectation, however, is that women will spend more time with infants and children than men will. Worse, there is often a socially-sanctioned suspicion that men are "not good" for young people to be around. As a result, most males, once they reach a certain age, are systematically denied opportunities to be close to young people (even after they become fathers).

GOAL

Organize against and eliminate the notion that men are not good for young people to be around, and actively promote the idea that males inherently want to be close to young people and will want to participate in children's growing up.

STRATEGIES

a) Hold out that courage, kindness, power, and gentleness are all *human* qualities, not accepting that "nature" has apportioned some qualities primarily to women and some to men. Men are inherently qualified to be caretakers and allies of children, and inherently desire to do so. A firm stand for achieving these positions will eventually garner widespread support.

b) Assist all men to discharge any feelings of separateness from or lack of interest in young people and their lives. Provide resource to men so that they can be intelligently loving and close to the children in their lives. Eliminate any economic or social structure that keeps men from being actively engaged in parenting or schoolteaching.

The "Mental Health" System

The "mental health" system is full of good people who have been trying to be useful in the struggles of people mis-defined as "mentally ill." However, this structure generally lacks an understanding of the nature of distress patterns and the discharge process, and has been largely taken over by profit motives. The "mental health" system plays a number of oppressive roles. Importantly, it is used as a threat in the inhibition of discharge, in the general enforcement of conformity, and in the destructive use of "shock-treatment," as well as dangerous and damaging drugs.

GOAL

We seek to transform the "mental health" system into a system effectively aiding complete discharge of men's distress, freeing men completely from distress recordings, and promoting the liberation of all humans, including men.

STRATEGIES

Re-introduce people working in the "mental health" system to the natural healing process of discharge and re-evaluation, and assist "mental health" workers to support men to reclaim the discharge processes. Educate "mental health" system workers in the reality of men's lives and men's oppression. Change the "mental health" system from a system based on profit and greed to a system based on healing, from a "professional" system to a human community.

Circumcision and Other Forms of Ritual Mutilation

Circumcision and other painful ordeals are inflicted on male infants and young men by religious, cultural, or medical institutions as "rites of initiation," with a number of rationalizations. These practices are possible only in the presence of beliefs that the males either do not suffer or that the suffering and damage are relatively unimportant.

GOAL

Promote and establish the concept that male circumcision is *abuse*, and eliminate it.

STRATEGIES

Inform people about the pain experienced by boys during circumcision, and the distress recordings that result from circumcision. Organize all people, especially targeting parents and medical personnel, to eliminate circumcision and all other forms of ritual mutilation of men, such as scarification and tattooing.

The Mass Media

The mass media, including TV shows, movies, and news programs, present damaging versions of men. Men are portrayed as rarely to be trusted to act human. Many are represented as completely evil (stalkers, rapists, terrorists, etc.). Others are portrayed as "stupid buffoons." Even male "heroes" are often given one-sided and simplified characterizations. (Advancing the appreciation of women in public entertainment is not accomplished by degrading the public representations of men in the same entertainment.)

GOAL

Transform the mass media into a force that communicates the *reality* about men and all human beings instead of the *distresses*, and into a force for human liberation, education, and communication.

STRATEGIES

Encourage presentations of men in the media that include the reality of their humanness and the real conditions of their lives. Include in the portrayal of male hero figures their struggles and their use of the discharge processes.

Women's Contribution to Men's Liberation

One consequence of men's role in the oppression of women is that women can find it difficult to see the basic goodness and humanness of men. This supports the oppression of men in an indirect way. Once women have been assisted in discharging their difficulties in seeing the true nature of men, they will become powerful allies in contradicting men's oppression on a broad scale. Men and women are natural allies for each other.

GOAL

Call for an alliance of all women with all men in which each is completely respected, and do the organizing work needed to bring this about.

STRATEGIES

Encourage women to lead men and men to follow women's leadership, especially in those areas (listed in this draft policy) where women have not been subjected to the same kind of distortion of their humanness as men have. Seek and welcome support from women, and plan on adopting an attitude of humility as an antidote to the sexism with which men have previously been contaminated. Seek to share the full disclosure of our respective richnesses.